*sparkteach

TEACHING THE CLASSICS TO TODAY'S STUDENTS

A Midsummer Night's Dream

WILLIAM SHAKESPEARE

*sparknotes FOR TEACHERS™

✳sparkteach

SPARKTEACH and the distinctive SparkTeach logo
are registered trademarks of SparkNotes LLC

© 2020 SparkNotes LLC
This 2020 edition printed for SparkNotes LLC by Sterling Publishing Co., Inc.

ISBN 978-1-4114-7994-4

Distributed in Canada by Sterling Publishing Co., Inc.
C/o Canadian Manda Group, 664 Annette Street
Toronto, Ontario M6S 2C8, Canada
Distributed in the United Kingdom by GMC Distribution Services
Castle Place, 166 High Street, Lewes, East Sussex BN7 1XU, England
Distributed in Australia by NewSouth Books
University of New South Wales, Sydney, NSW 2052, Australia

For information about custom editions, special sales, and premium
and corporate purchases, please contact Sterling Special Sales at
800-805-5489 or specialsales@sterlingpublishing.com.

Manufactured in Canada

2 4 6 8 10 9 7 5 3 1

sparkteach.com
sparknotes.com
sterlingpublishing.com

Cover design by Elizabeth Mihaltse Lindy
Cover and title page illustration by MUTI
Interior design by Kevin Ullrich
IMAGE CREDITS iStock/Getty Images Plus/filborg: 14, 15;
Library of Congress: 60; shutterstock.com: agsandrew: 61; Gimas: 43;
courtesy of Wikimedia Commons: 59

Contents

PART 1
Welcome to SparkTeach!

SparkTeach is a unique set of teaching guides and lesson plans designed to help make classic literature engaging and relevant to today's students.

We asked teachers about the biggest challenges they face in their English classes, and their answer was clear: "We need to engage our students, spark their interest in literature, and make our lessons relevant." That's why we developed SparkTeach, customizable materials including teaching frameworks, lessons, in-class worksheets, and more for the most popular titles taught today!

The following pages provide you with helpful tips for lesson planning and classroom management, an explanation of each component, including a detailed description of a "Real-Life Lens Lesson"; an explanation of the role of the ELA Common Core State Standards in the program; and guidelines for student assessment.

SparkTeach materials are easily customizable and can be adapted for many different learning styles. We encourage you to utilize the lessons as best fits your classroom's needs.

Tips for Class Planning and Management

Here are some tips for planning and managing your class as students work their way through a SparkTeach unit. To maximize student learning and engagement:

1. Preview SparkTeach Materials

Review all the materials available for a text. Decide which worksheets you will use based on student needs. You may choose materials to match a particular text in your curriculum, or you may assign a text after being inspired by a specific Real-Life Lens Lesson.

2. Gather Your Materials

Once you've selected the components you'll need, preview each lesson and then download and print all of the chosen worksheets. Be sure to print out enough copies for each student and one copy for yourself to use as reference. Hand out all worksheets needed prior to reading, such as Contextual Support Handouts, as these promote student comprehension.

If the Real-Life Lens Lesson or Film Lesson requires a specific film, make sure to have the film on hand to show the class. If specific scene timestamps are provided, preview the scenes so that you will feel prepared to answer students' questions.

Review the Midpoint Activities and Final Project options in the Real-Life Lens Lesson. Will you need specific equipment such as a video recorder or a printer for students to complete a project? Be sure your students will have access to the tools they'll need to complete their work.

3. Set Your Schedule

Once you've chosen a Real-Life Lens Lesson, read it through before starting. Choose your start, midpoint, and end dates to keep on schedule. Each framework should take multiple class periods to complete; plan each activity and project accordingly. Will students need access to the school library or the internet to conduct research for their final projects? If so, be sure to schedule time for student research, review, and revision.

4. Preview Real-Life Links

Read, watch, or listen to each of the Real-Life Links. Decide which resources will engage your students the most. Prepare a few questions to use to ignite student thinking, guide quick written responses, and initiate class discussion.

5. Monitor Student Progress and Comprehension

Routinely schedule one-on-one meetings with students to check their comprehension and progress throughout reading. During group work or discussions, circulate around the room to monitor student collaboration and communication and to gently guide discussions back on topic, if necessary. Recording your observations and assessments will enable you to note individual and whole-class progress as work continues.

6. Let Students Shine

Schedule plenty of time for all students to present their final projects. They have worked hard all month, and showing off their finished work boosts confidence and allows students to see the unique and creative ways their peers interpreted and approached a similar topic.

7. Personalize Content

Real-Life Lens Lessons are designed to ensure students engage with each text in a meaningful way. Lenses are specially chosen to help students connect with even the most challenging texts on a personal level. As you progress through the materials, look for ways to help students relate the text to their own lives. Notice what excites them and tailor your lessons accordingly.

What's Included in SparkTeach?

Real-Life Lens Lessons

The Real-Life Lens Lesson is a unit that focuses on a specific text over multiple class periods. The driving force behind each unit is the lens, a carefully selected theme through which students view the text. This lens provides students with a relatable point of entry. A thorough explanation of each feature in a Real-Life Lens Lesson is detailed in the next section beginning on page 8. Each Real-Life Lens Lesson includes several downloadable worksheets and assessment materials to round out the unit.

Reading Skills Worksheets

Each set of teaching materials features multiple Reading Skills Worksheets designed to help develop the ELA reading skills outlined in the Common Core State Standards. Worksheets engage students in a variety of activities that deepen understanding of both the skill and the featured text. Each worksheet is printable.

Vocabulary Builders

Each set of teaching materials also includes at least one Vocabulary Builder based on the specific language found in the text. You can pass out the builder prior to starting the text and refer to it as students read to ensure comprehension. Other builders ask students to engage with the vocabulary through graphic organizers, charts, or other activities. Each builder is printable.

Contextual Support Handouts

To aid comprehension, each set of teaching materials features at least one Contextual Support handout to provide information to students about topics relevant to the text. Student comprehension is hindered if historical or background information is unknown or not clear. We developed these handouts to arm students with the information they'll need to better understand each text.

Poetics Lessons

Understanding poetic devices helps students comprehend classic and modern texts and appreciate a writer's choices and craft. Each poetics lesson provides an in-depth exploration of a key poetic device, such as metaphor or simile. Each lesson features examples from the literary text that demonstrate the topic and provides a foundation from which students can work. These lessons come with printable student-facing worksheets and sample answers.

Film Lessons

When teaching Shakespeare, it's good to remember that the works were intended to be acted out by players and viewed by an audience, not read as literature. Students can benefit greatly and process these texts most effectively by experiencing Shakespeare's plays visually. Film productions of Shakespeare's plays provide a wealth of learning opportunities. We designed SparkTeach Film Lessons to help connect Shakespearean texts with a modern audience and help students—especially visual learners—engage with the texts in a new way. These lessons also allow for more differentiation in the classroom and deepen students' understanding of the plays. Each lesson comes with downloadable student-facing worksheets and sample answers.

What Makes Real-Life Lens Lessons Unique?

Real-Life Lens Lessons, the hub of SparkTeach materials, set this literature program apart. Each Real-Life Lens Lesson is thoughtfully designed to help students view the text—even older or more challenging works—through a relatable lens that enables students to connect with the text in a meaningful way. A powerful teaching tool, each teacher-facing Real-Life Lens Lesson provides a framework for organizing and executing a unit over multiple class periods that focuses on a particular work of literature. Each element found in a Real-Life Lens Lesson is listed and described below.

1. The Lens

The lens is the heart of each Real-Life Lens Lesson. The lens shapes classroom discussions, student analysis, and all lesson activities and projects. The lens invites students to explore the text in a way that connects the content with their own lives—their experiences, concerns, interests, and aspirations.

Introduce the Lens Through Real-Life Links

- Each Real-Life Lens Lesson features several Real-Life Links including online articles, podcasts, videos, and surveys.

- Real-Life Links are meant to be shared with students prior to or during reading.

- After students read, listen to, or watch the Real-Life Links, but before reading of the text begins, the class participates in an activity designed to introduce the lens to students in a meaningful way.

2. Big Idea Questions

- The Big Idea Questions are overarching questions that provide students with a base from which to start thinking about the text. For example: "What is reality, and how do we know what is real?" (See page 15.)

- Students are encouraged to return to these questions as they read and note how their answers to the questions change over the course of the unit.

3. Driving Questions

In addition to the Big Idea Questions, each Real-Life Lens Lesson contains a number of Driving Questions. Unlike the Big Idea Questions, Driving Questions are more specific in their focus and are designed to guide student exploration of the text, as related to the lens. Some examples of Driving Questions featured in *A Midsummer Night's Dream* include:

- What happens to the characters' perceptions of reality while they are in the forest?

- What "truths" are revealed about the characters while in the forest?

- Why do you think Shakespeare chooses dreams as a literary device?

4. Differentiated Instruction

- To ensure all students can access learning, we have provided differentiated instruction for all Midpoint Activities and final projects.

- Suggestions for increasing and/or decreasing the difficulty of each activity and project are found throughout each Real-Life Lens Lesson.

5. Midpoint Activities

- Two engaging Midpoint Activities are featured to ensure student comprehension of the text and give you an opportunity to assess learning.

- These activities encourage students to consolidate their understanding of the text so far and challenge them to use that understanding to make predictions about the rest of the text and analyze what they know of the plot, characters, or theme.

6. Paired Text Recommendations

- Our list of paired text recommendations suggests contemporary novels you can pair with the classic novel you're teaching.

- Students can connect to passages from multiple novels by comparing, contrasting, and analyzing the works side by side.

7. Final Projects

- Each Real-Life Lens Lesson presents students with two options for final projects that encapsulate what they have learned about the text as seen through the lens.

- Students are invited to choose the project that excites them the most at the beginning of the unit and to keep this project in mind as they read.

- These dynamic projects are designed to provide opportunities for students to demonstrate their mastery of the text in creative and fun ways.

- Examples of projects include creating a multimedia presentation or video, rewriting and performing a scene from the text, and participating in a formal debate on a specific issue.

8. Supporting Worksheets and Graphic Organizers

- Each Real-Life Lens Lesson offers several printable worksheets, including a **Driving Questions Worksheet, located on page 83,** on which students can record answers as they read, and graphic organizers to support student learning.

- To save you time and help students understand how to tackle each task, each worksheet includes scaffolded directions and a sample student response if necessary.

9. Student and Teacher Reflection Worksheets

- The **Student Reflection Worksheet, located on page 96,** encourages students to assess their strengths, weaknesses, and level of engagement throughout the Real-Life Lens Lesson.

- Self-assessment cultivates confidence, as students note how they worked through challenges; nurtures good study habits; and encourages students to take responsibility for their own learning.

- The **Teacher Reflection Worksheet, located on page 97,** allows you to evaluate what elements of the unit students found the most engaging, where they seemed to struggle, and what approaches or elements worked the best for you and your class.

SparkTeach and the Common Core State Standards

Every component included in SparkTeach was developed to ensure broad coverage of the ELA Common Core State Standards. Materials were designed to provide multiple opportunities for your students to address a wide variety of Reading Literature, Speaking and Listening, Writing, and Language standards.

Each standard addressed by an activity, discussion, or project is listed for easy reference so that you can track which standards each lesson or worksheet covers.

Guidelines for Student Assessment

Each set of SparkTeach materials provides extensive assessment opportunities, including a **Rubric for Student Assessment, a Student Reflection Worksheet, and a Teacher Reflection Worksheet (see pages 92–97)**. Use these assets, along with lesson-specific assessment advice within each Real-Life Lens Lesson, to successfully gauge student learning.

Worksheet Assessment

Many Reading Skills Worksheets and Vocabulary Builders may be scored in a traditional fashion. To make grading easier and faster, we have provided full answer keys for worksheets that contain clear correct or incorrect answers and sample student answers for worksheets that require more subjective, open-ended answers.

Real-Life Lens Lesson Assessment

Each Real-Life Lens Lesson offers opportunities for informal, formal, and self-assessment. Performance assessment involves observing student collaboration, while formal assessment entails grading a writing assignment, worksheet, or final project.

PART 2

SparkTeach
A Midsummer Night's Dream
Lesson Plans

Real-Life Lens Lesson
Dreams and Reality

Use this Real-Life Lens Lesson to help students dive deep into Shakespeare's *A Midsummer Night's Dream* and examine the play's themes, action, and characters through the lens of dreams and reality. How do dreams offer an enhanced, or distorted, version of reality? How do they reveal our emotions or desires (or do they)? What is the role of dreaming in this play, and how does it relate to other major themes like love, marriage, gender, and friendship?

Materials

A Midsummer Night's Dream by William Shakespeare

Worksheets: Driving Questions, page 83

The Dream in the Forest, page 85

Introduce the Lens

To activate students' thinking, choose one or two of the following Real-Life Links to use in an engagement activity. Have students read or watch and discuss the content. Encourage students to jot down notes, or record class notes on the board for future reference.

Real-Life Links: Dreams and Reality

Why Do We Dream?

In this TEDEd animated video, educator Amy Adkins explores the top seven reasons why we might dream.

https://ed.ted.com/lessons/why-do-we-dream-amy-adkins

The Science Behind Dreaming

In this *Scientific American* article, psychology researcher Sander van der Linden details recent scientific observations of the mechanisms behind dreaming and the relationship between dreams and memories.

https://www.scientificamerican.com/article/the-science-behind-dreaming/

A Few of the Many Ways We Distort Reality

In this *Psychology Today* article, Karyn Hall, PhD, explains how and why we distort reality and offers advice on how we can alter our thinking to see reality as it is, not as we think it is.

https://www.psychologytoday.com/us/blog/pieces-mind/201208/few-the-many-ways-we-distort-reality

Social Construction of Reality

This SparkNotes article provides a review of the widely accepted idea that reality is different for each individual, also known as the Social Construction of Reality theory.

https://www.sparknotes.com/sociology/identity-and-reality/section1/

Do We See Reality as It Is?

In this TEDEd Talk, cognitive scientist Donald Hoffman lays out a detailed exploration of the question of the degree to which our minds construct reality for us.

https://www.ted.com/talks/donald_hoffman_do_we_see_reality_as_it_is/discussion?referrer=playlist-how_your_brain_constructs_real

Pose the Following Big Idea Questions to the Class:

What is reality, and how do we know what is real?
How do dreams both enhance and defy reality?

Engagement Activity

- Have students write quick initial answers to the questions.

- Discuss the questions, either as a class or in small groups. Prompt students to consider the relationship between dreams and reality.

- Encourage students to think about both how dreams differ from reality and how they reflect it.

- Following discussion, give students time to revise their initial responses and ask volunteers to share what they wrote with the class.

CCSS: SL.11-12.1

Introduce the Driving Questions

Begin by having students write their own questions about the lesson topic. Encourage them to think about what they already know about the lens of dreams and reality and what they're interested in exploring further.

Hand out the **Driving Questions Worksheet, located on page 83**. Review the questions as a class. Students should enter initial answers to the questions as they read *A Midsummer Night's Dream*. They will revisit the questions and revise their answers following the lesson activities, classroom discussion, and completion of the text. Remind students to support their responses with text evidence.

Integrate the Driving Questions into your classroom discussions. Use them to help guide students' thinking about the Big Idea Questions.

1. What happens to the characters' perceptions of reality while they are in the forest?
2. Who is under the spell of the love potion? Who isn't? Why might this be significant?
3. What does the love potion symbolize? How does it link dreams and reality?
4. What "truths" are revealed about the characters while in the forest?
5. How does Shakespeare set up an opposition between the city and the forest, and how does this relate to the theme of reality and illusion in the play?
6. How does dreaming function as both a disruptive and unifying force in the play?
7. What are Theseus's views on love and rationality, and how are they similar to or different from Hermia's?
8. How do Theseus's and Hermia's views together form a "complete" commentary on reality in the play?
9. Why do you think Shakespeare chooses dreams as a literary device?

Introduce the "Through the Lens" Activity

Activity: Personal Experience

In this activity, students will discuss their own dreams and how they are/are not linked to reality.

Ask students to write a paragraph about a dream they have had and how it related to their real life. (If you feel that students might be uncomfortable writing about their dreams, have them write about another person's dream they heard about or a dream of a character in a story or film.) In their paragraphs, students should note what happened in the dream, what emotions they experienced while dreaming and after they woke up, and how the dream might have related to anything that was going on in their lives at the time.

Pair students and have partners share their paragraphs. Encourage pairs to return to the Big Idea Questions and consider how their experiences informed their initial answers.

Invite three or four students to share their paragraphs with the class. Prompt whole-class discussion with questions, such as: *Was the dream a pleasant dream or a nightmare? What emotions did you experience during the dream and after waking? What kinds of things happened in the dream that could not happen in real life? What events or experiences were you going through at the time? Can you relate the dream to any of them?*

Before moving on, explain that students will explore Shakespeare's treatment of dreams and their powerful effects through his use of characterization, plot, and language as they read *A Midsummer Night's Dream*.

Differentiated Instruction

This activity can be modified to help all students access learning.

Decrease Difficulty

Begin by having students define what dreams are. Then, rather than having all students write about a personal experience, ask two or three volunteers to describe their experiences orally to the class. Proceed with discussion as outlined above, including more students.

Increase Difficulty

Have students write short personal essays about an experience of dreaming. Ask two or three students to read their essays to the class and proceed with discussion as outlined above.

Introduce the Final Project

Before moving on, introduce the final projects to the class (see pages 20–21). Have students choose the project they will complete and encourage them to keep their project in mind as they read the text. Facilitate the formation of project groups if necessary.

Assign the Midpoint Activities

Activity 1: Characterization: Dream Scene

Students will analyze a scene from the dream sequence in the play (Act 3, scene 2) and infer what each character's dream reveals about him or her. Before the activity begins, pass out **The Dream in the Forest Worksheet, located on page 85**. Students will:

- review Act 3, scene 2

- complete the worksheet with details from the scene to:
    - analyze each character's language and actions to infer what this "dreaming state" reveals about the character's main conflict and potential innermost fears and desires.

    - compare the character's language and actions before entering the dream sequence (i.e., before entering the forest), while in the dream sequence (in the forest), and after the dream sequence (out of the forest).

- write an essay or develop an oral presentation to present their analyses, as you prefer for your class.

CCSS: RL.11-12.1, RL.11-12.3, SL.11-12.2, W.11-12.1

Differentiated Instruction

Decrease Difficulty

Have students work in pairs to complete the worksheet. Then, rather than assigning essays, lead a class discussion in which each pair shares information from their completed worksheet.

Increase Difficulty

As part of their oral presentations, have each student develop a performance of one character's soliloquy that supports their analysis of the text.

Activity 2: Make Predictions

Students will make predictions about what will occur in the remainder of the play based on an analysis of the dream sequence (Act 3, scene 2). Students will:

- create a summary of the major plot events of the dream sequence. This can be done in note form or as a more formal written summary, as best suits your class.

- write at least three predictions about what will occur in the final acts of the play based on their summaries.

- return to their predictions when they have finished reading the text and confirm or correct their predictions.

Paired Text Recommendations

Encourage students to read passages from contemporary novels that similarly feature the theme of dreams and reality. In pairing multiple texts with similar themes, students are challenged to look beyond the book they're studying and find new ways to connect to the themes. Here are some books you can pair with *A Midsummer Night's Dream*:

- *Dreamers Often Lie* by Jacqueline West

- *This Must Be Love* by Tui T. Sutherland

- *Wondrous Strange* by Lesley Livingston

Final Projects

Students will work on their final projects after they have finished reading the complete text of *A Midsummer Night's Dream*. Project 1 can be completed by students working individually, while Project 2 calls for small groups.

> **CCSS: RL.11-12.1, RL.11-12.2, W.11-12.1**

Final Project 1: Dream Machine

Students will work individually to analyze one character and his or her desires and romantic relationship based on what happens to the character before going into the forest, while in the forest, and after leaving the forest. Students will use their analysis to create a dream the character may (or may not) have for his or her future. Students will:

- summarize the main conflict the character faces and main events that happen to the character.

- summarize the character's viewpoints on relationships and love, as well as his or her values in general.

- create a new dream for the character, as if the character were to return to the forest under the influence of the love potion, based on their summaries.

- present their findings and created dream in an essay.

Differentiated Instruction

Decrease Difficulty

Have students work in pairs. Have each student responsible for a specific portion of the essay, thus reducing the amount of writing any one student will have to produce. Have partners exchange essay portions for editing and feedback before they assemble a final essay.

Increase Difficulty

Have students assemble a collage (print or digital) that reflects the atmosphere of the dream they have created for their characters. Students should carefully consider color, images, and even accompanying music and be prepared to explain their choices to the class.

Final Project 2: Dreams versus Reality

Small groups will choose a dream sequence scene in the play and create two sets of cartoon panels representing an event from the dream sequence: one cartoon should reflect the "reality" of the event (as a bystander or the reader would perceive the events), and the other cartoon should represent the "dream reality" as perceived by the dreaming character(s). Students will work together to:

- craft two cartoon strips containing at least three panels each that detail the major plot points of the chosen dream sequence. Students can use paper and colored pencils or design software.

- include a two- to three-line explanation below each panel that will, when paired with the cartoon, summarize the dream sequence.

- consider color, design, and other styling elements to portray the mood, emotion, and tone for each set of panels.

- write an explanation or give a short oral presentation of their panels, which includes a rationale behind design choices made and how these choices relate to the themes of dreaming and reality in the play.

Differentiated Instruction

Decrease Difficulty

Help groups assign project roles so that all students are performing tasks within their abilities. Before groups begin working, review what effective communication and collaboration entail.

Increase Difficulty

Have students research set designs, direction, and actors who have performed this play on stage or in film to compare these choices with their rationales. Have groups produce brief statements that summarize what they learn through their research.

Assess the Assignments

Use the **Rubric for Student Assessment, located on page 92,** to evaluate student work on the lesson assignments.

Distribute the **Student Reflection Worksheet, located on page 96**. Guide students through the self-assessment and reflection questions.

Complete the **Teacher Reflection Worksheet, located on page 97**. Record which elements of the lesson plan worked well for your class and which elements you might revise for future classes.

Poetics Lesson

Poetic Meter and Social Class in
A Midsummer Night's Dream

Lesson Overview

Students will identify poetic meter in William Shakespeare's *A Midsummer Night's Dream* and explain how and to what effect Shakespeare uses poetic meter to create contrast between social classes and to create meaning in the text. This lesson can be completed as students read the text or once they have finished reading.

Materials

A Midsummer Night's Dream by William Shakespeare

Worksheet: Poetic Meter and Social Class, page 86

Lesson Objectives

1. Students will analyze the purpose and function of language forms in texts.
2. Students will identify poetic meter and prose in *A Midsummer Night's Dream* and understand how they are used to create contrast among social classes.
3. Students will scan lines to identify variations in meter and examine how they are used to create meaning.

Instructional Sequence

1. Convey the purpose of poetic meter.

In reading works of literature, it is essential to understand not only the form a work is written in but also how that form is used to create meaning in the text. Put simply, writers shape meaning through not only *what* they are saying in the text but also *how* they express it. Shakespeare, in particular, is known for using meter to express what might not be immediately apparent about a character or a situation, particularly through his variation in meter. Variation in meter, in essence, is the hallmark of poetic meaning.

2. Define poetic meter and iambic pentameter.

- **Poetic meter is rhythmic pattern in language, a key component of verse, or poetry.**
- **Rhythmic patterns in language (for the most part) are created by patterns of stressed and unstressed syllables called feet.**

There are dozens of poetic meters in literature, each defined by their own particular pattern of stressed and unstressed syllables. For example, examine the following lines from *A Midsummer Night's Dream*.

HIPPOLYTA
  Four days will quickly steep themselves in night.
  Four nights will quickly dream away the time.
  (*No Fear*: 1.1.7–8)

In these lines, there are five pairs of syllables, or feet, that follow an unstressed-stressed pattern (the stressed syllables appear in bold):

HIPPOLYTA
  Four **days**/ will **qui**/ ckly **steep**/ them **selves**/ in **night**.
  Four **nights**/ will **qui**/ ckly **dream**/ a **way**/ the **time**.

This rhythmic pattern is called *iambic pentameter*.

Iambic pentameter has five (penta = five) pairs of iambic feet, or iambs (a pair of unstressed-stressed syllables) for a total of ten syllables per line. Iambic pentameter is the meter that Shakespeare most used to write his plays.

Practice reading the lines aloud with students, emphasizing the stressed syllables. Have students clap for stresses or stomp their feet to better "feel" the rhythm of the verse.

3. Discuss how to identify verse versus prose.

All *verse* is written with meter and is poetic in nature and content. *Prose*, in contrast, is language that is not written with any special meter.

Shakespeare wrote *A Midsummer Night's Dream* (as well as other plays) in a mix of verse and prose. It is important for students to be able to distinguish when Shakespeare is using verse and when he is using prose in his plays.

Whereas verse can be divided by rhythmic units of stressed and unstressed syllables, prose is usually only divided by grammatical units. Verse can either rhyme or not rhyme, but if the language follows a metrical pattern, it's verse.

One of the easiest ways for students to identify verse and prose in Shakespeare's plays is to examine how the text is laid out on the page. Verse will begin each line with a capital letter, even when sentences carry over onto the next line. Prose will not (unless the sentences happen to line up that way). Prose appears as a paragraph; the sentences flow across the page. Shakespeare's prose might not have the tight meter and patterning that his verse does, but it is still rich in tone and figurative language.

4. Identify verse and prose selections.

Have each student identify a verse passage and a prose passage from the text. The passages should be no fewer than four lines each. Students may have to scan more than one act to find examples of each.

Before having students scan, to support their understanding, copy these passages on the board for practice with the class. Have students turn to the passages in their texts as well.

HERMIA
   So I will grow, so live, so die, my lord,
   Ere I will yield my virgin patent up
   Unto his Lordship, whose unwished yoke
   My soul consents not to give sovereignty.
   (*No Fear*: 1.1.79–82)

BOTTOM
   I grant you, friends, if you should fright the ladies out of their wits, they would have no
   more discretion but to hang us. But I will aggravate my voice so that I will roar you as
   gently as any sucking dove.
   (*No Fear*: 1.2.33–34)

Have students analyze how each passage is laid out. Have a volunteer come to the board and underline or circle where the lines are capitalized.

HERMIA
   So I will grow, so live, so die, my lord,
   Ere I will yield my virgin patent up

Unto his Lordship, whose unwished yoke
My soul consents not to give sovereignty.
(*No Fear*: 1.1.79–82)

BOTTOM

I grant you, friends, if you should fright the ladies out of their wits, they would have no more discretion but to hang us. But I will aggravate my voice so that I will roar you as gently as any sucking dove.
(*No Fear*: 1.2.33–34)

Students should determine that the first passage is verse, since each line begins with a capital letter, and the second is prose, since each line is not capitalized and complete sentences extend across the page.

5. Note the effects.

As a class, discuss the effects of each use of language. Discuss who is speaking each of these lines. For example, the first set of lines is spoken by Hermia, who is nobility, and the second set of lines is spoken by Bottom, who is a commoner. Discuss the effects of using these different types of language for each character and what Shakespeare might have been trying to express or signal to the audience by using verse for Hermia and prose for Bottom.

6. Scan any verse to identify poetic meter.

Return to the verse passage copied on the board. Scan the lines with students to identify the stressed and unstressed syllables. Read the lines slowly out loud for students. Show students how to mark the passage. Above stressed syllables use a (') symbol. Above unstressed syllables use a (u) symbol. Use the (/) symbol to indicate the boundaries between feet.

So I/will grow, so live/so die, my lord,
Ere I/will yield/my virgin patent up
Unto/his lordship, whose/unwished yoke
My soul/consents/not to/give sovereignty. (1.1.79-82)

Have students mark the passage in their books along with you. Count the total number of feet in each line and write the number beside the end of each line. *Note: There are five feet in each line*. Guide students to see that the lines are written in five pairs of unstressed-stressed syllables. Remind students that these pairs of syllables are called iambs, and since there are five of them, the meter is iambic pentameter.

Be aware that other poetic meters exist in the play, and students might come across these as they analyze the lines for meter. For example, Shakespeare uses *trochaic tetrameter* at the end of the play when Robin/Puck addresses the audience (*No Fear*: 5.1.406–411).

Trochaic tetrameter is a type of meter in poetry in which each line contains four trochaic feet, each made of one stressed syllable, followed by an unstressed syllable.

7. Notice variations in poetic meter and their effects.

Note with students when they are encountering a simple variation in poetic meter or another poetic meter altogether. One way to help identify the difference is noticing whether a variation in pattern *persists* in a passage—this usually signals that another meter is being used. For example, if the lines consistently contain eight syllables rather than ten, then the meter is likely not iambic pentameter. If only a few lines are shorter, then a variation might be intentional and being used to express something about the situation or character. For example, in Act 3, scene 2, one of Hermia's lines is only five syllables long instead of ten. This shortened line is used to express Hermia's rage at Helena, who she believes is making fun of her. Have students find this line, and then other variations in rhythm and stresses in the passages.

8. Complete the worksheet.

Pass out the **Poetic Meter and Social Class Worksheet, located on page 86**. Have students complete the worksheet. If necessary, review the sample answers as a class.

CCSS: RL.11-12.1, RL.11-12.2, RL.11-12.3, RL.11-12.4

Differentiated Instruction

This activity can be modified to help all students access learning.

Decrease Difficulty

Choose two passages from the text that all students will work with to complete the chart.

As a class, identify the character, social class, and type of language used in each passage.

Have students work in pairs to analyze the effect Shakespeare creates by using this type of language for this character.

Review students' answers as a class and extend the discussion to cover the purpose of each type of language.

Increase Difficulty

Have students find and add a passage that uses trochaic tetrameter to the chart.

As a class, discuss why Shakespeare might have used this type of meter for this character (e.g., "Trochaic tetrameter has a more sing-song feel, which is why it might have been used for the fairies, who are magical and joyous").

Film Lesson
Themes in Michael Hoffman's *A Midsummer Night's Dream*

In this lesson, students will compare scenes in the text of *A Midsummer Night's Dream* with scenes in the 1999 film by director Michael Hoffman to better understand how themes are expressed in the play and the film.

When directors create an adaptation of a movie, they have many choices to make beyond just casting and scenery. They might consider questions such as: *Which virtues or flaws of a character could be emphasized for effect through imagery or dialogue? How does one create emotional depth in a character through visuals and sound? What elements can be changed to highlight and promote certain themes over others?* A director's answers to these questions can determine whether the film is a fresh, engaging adaptation or one that falls flat.

For this lesson, students will first review the key themes of *A Midsummer Night's Dream*. Then, they will watch Michael Hoffman's 1999 film. While watching the film, students will look closely for differences in the ways Hoffman expresses the play's major themes by comparing any differences in character, dialogue, imagery, setting, and other devices in each of the scenes in the movie with the same scene in the text.

Materials

A Midsummer Night's Dream by William Shakespeare

Worksheet: Themes in Hoffman's Film, page 88

A Midsummer Night's Dream directed by Michael Hoffman, Fox Searchlight Pictures, 1999

Lesson Objectives

1. Students will review and briefly discuss the key themes in *A Midsummer Night's Dream*.
2. Students will identify the different ways the play's key themes are expressed in Hoffman's *A Midsummer Night's Dream* versus in the text.

Instructional Sequence

This activity is designed to be completed after students have read all of *A Midsummer Night's Dream* by William Shakespeare.

1. Pass out the worksheet **Themes in Hoffman's Film, located on page 88.**

2. As a class, review the major themes of the play listed in the first column of the chart. Ask students which plot points they can recall that reflect these themes. Then, in the second column, instruct students to jot down different scenes from the text that deal with each theme. They can look through their text as necessary. For now, students should only note the act and scene from the text in which this theme is explored. They will record additional details here after watching the film.

3. Review the sample answer in the first row with students to prepare them to complete the chart as they watch. Then present Hoffman's film to the class. Remind students to pay close attention to the scenes they recorded and how these scenes are presented in the movie. Have them record any differences in the scenes in the film compared to the text in the second and third columns of the chart.

4. Instruct students to jot down any other general differences they notice between the text and film on the other side of their worksheet.

5. After students have watched the film, have them return to their worksheets and, in the fourth column, describe the overall effect the differences between the text and the film have on their understanding of the theme. Ask: *What effects do Hoffman's changes create? What do you think Hoffman's purpose was in creating these changes? Do the changes enhance your understanding of the theme or hinder it? Do these changes "work"? Why or why not?*

6. As a class or in small groups, have students share their findings and interpretations.

Here are some differences from the text to watch for in the film:

- The action is set in Monte Athena, Italy, during the late-nineteenth-century Victorian era rather than sixteenth-century Athens, Greece.

- Bicycles are used by the characters to escape and serve as a symbol of youth and progress in the movie. Fog appears from the bike as Robin/Puck leaves at the end of the play.

- Bottom has a wife in the movie; there is no mention of a wife in the play.

- Bottom is wearing a crown Titania gives him when he wakes from his dream.

- Helena and Hermia's fight involves a mud pit in the movie; there is no mud pit in the play.

CCSS: RL.11-12.3, RL.11-12.7

Differentiated Instruction

This activity can be modified to help all students access learning.

Decrease Difficulty

Before students watch the movie, choose one theme from the worksheet, and complete the second column together. Then, have students work in pairs to complete the worksheets as they watch. Stop the film when key scenes arise.

Increase Difficulty

Have students write a review of the movie. Have students focus their essay on whether Hoffman was successful or not in expressing the themes in the play with his choices by discussing two or three changes Hoffman made and analyzing their effects.

PART 3

Worksheets and Handouts

Shakespeare Speak

Overview

Some of the words and phrases Shakespeare uses are so uncommon today that they may sound like another language to the modern reader. This can be discouraging for students as they struggle with Elizabethan vocabulary that inhibits their understanding of a play. Becoming familiar with "Shakespeare speak" will help students to better understand his works and build confidence when studying Shakespeare. Students will use this worksheet to examine and learn common vocabulary used in many of Shakespeare's plays. They will read a term in context, write a definition from that context, and then find a definition from another source.

RL.9-10.4 Determine the meaning of words and phrases as they are used in the text, including figurative and connotative meanings; analyze the cumulative impact of specific word choices on meaning and tone (e.g., how the language evokes a sense of time and place; how it sets a formal or informal tone).

Shakespeare Speak

Some of the words and phrases Shakespeare uses are so uncommon today that they may sound like another language to the modern reader. Yet these terms were commonly used during his day. Becoming familiar with "Shakespeare speak" will help you to better understand his works.

Study the list of words taken from some of Shakespeare's most well-known plays. Read the section of the play in which each word is used. Based on the context, define the word to the best of your ability. Record your definition in the third column. Then, after creating your own definition from the context, provide the dictionary definition in the fourth column. How close was your definition?

Word	Text from the Play	Your Definition Based on Context	Dictionary Definition
beguiled	"Poor ropes, you are beguiled, / Both you and I, for Romeo is exiled." (*No Fear Shakespeare Romeo and Juliet* 3.2.133–134)	tricked or fooled	hoodwinked, deceived (Webster's)
beseech	"I yet beseech your majesty, / If for I want that glib and oily art / To speak and purpose not—since what I well intend[.]" (*No Fear Shakespeare King Lear* 1.1.230–232)		
chide	"Do you not come your tardy son to chide. / That, lapsed in time and passion, lets go by / The important acting of your dread command?" (*No Fear Shakespeare Hamlet* 3.4.108–110)		
entreat	"I do entreat your grace to pardon me. / I know not by what power I am made bold / Nor how it may concern my modesty / In such a presence here to plead my thoughts[.]" (*No Fear Shakespeare A Midsummer Night's Dream* 1.1.58–61)		

*spark*teach **33**

Word	Text from the Play	Your Definition Based on Context	Dictionary Definition
canker	"To put down Richard, that sweet lovely rose. / An plant this thorn, this canker, Bolingbroke? / And shall it in more shame be further spoken / That you are fooled, discarded, and shook off / By him for whom these shames you underwent?" (*No Fear Shakespeare Henry IV, Part 1* 1.3.174–178)		
forsworn	"By my knavery (if I had it), then I were. But if you swear by that that is not, you are not forsworn[.]" (*No Fear Shakespeare As You Like It* 1.2.61–63)		
fortune	"Thou know'st that all my fortunes are at sea. / Neither have I money nor commodity / To raise a present sum." (*No Fear Shakespeare The Merchant of Venice* 1.1.179–181)		
haste	"Signior Baptista, my business asketh haste, / And every day I cannot come to woo." (*No Fear Shakespeare The Taming of the Shrew* 2.1.107–108)		
jest	"I knew him, Horatio, a fellow of infinite jest, of most excellent fancy." (*No Fear Shakespeare Hamlet* 5.1.160–161)		
shrift	"Be plain, good son, and homely in thy drift. / Riddling confession finds but riddling shrift." (*No Fear Shakespeare Romeo and Juliet* 2.3.55–56)		

Word	Text from the Play	Your Definition Based on Context	Dictionary Definition
shrive	"I should be glad of his approach. If he have the condition of a saint and the complexion of a devil, I had rather he should shrive me than wive me." (*No Fear Shakespeare The Merchant of Venice* 1.2.112–115)		
sojourn	"The two great princes, France and Burgundy, / Great rivals in our youngest daughter's love. / Long in our court have made their amorous sojourn[.]" (*No Fear Shakespeare King Lear* 1.1.44–46)		
herald	"It is the part of men to fear and tremble / When the most mighty gods by tokens send / Such dreadful heralds to astonish us." (*No Fear Shakespeare Julius Caesar* 1.3.55–57)		
woe	"If e'er thou wast thyself and these woes thine, / Thou and these woes were all for Rosaline." (*No Fear Shakespeare Romeo and Juliet* 2.3.77–78)		
wrought	"How you were borne in hand, how crossed, the instruments, / Who wrought with them, and all things else that might / To half a soul and to a notion crazed / Say, 'Thus did Banquo.'" (*No Fear Shakespeare Macbeth* 3.1.83–86)		

Archaic Language

Overview

Although the themes and emotions of Shakespeare's plays remain extraordinarily relevant to the modern student, the archaic language presents challenges to today's learners. This handout sets students up for success with Shakespeare's works by explaining commonly challenging archaic diction in Elizabethan English. Students will study definitions of common pronouns, verbs, and phrases and write modern synonyms to help increase their understanding and retention of what they read.

Archaic Language

Many people struggle with comprehension when reading Shakespeare's plays. One of the reasons for this is that our language has changed enormously since Shakespeare's time. There are many words, phrases, and terms that were in common use then that are no longer used today. There are also words that are still used today but with a different meaning. Words and meanings that have fallen out of common use are referred to as *archaic diction*.

Pronouns

One specific and potentially confusing grammatical element from Shakespeare's time is the use of different words for today's *you* and *your*. Archaic diction is often filled with unfamiliar pronouns, such as *thee* and *thine* and *thou* and *thy*, or familiar pronouns with different meanings, such as the word *you*.

Study the charts to familiarize yourself with common archaic terms.

Archaic Term	Modern Form	Archaic Usage Rule/Grammar
thou	you (singular)	more familiar and informal address, used as the subject of a sentence "Be as well neighbored, pitied, and relieved / As thou my sometime daughter." (*No Fear Shakespeare King Lear* 1.1.120–121)
you	you	more polite and formal address, used as the object of a sentence "And now, Laertes, what's the news with you?" (*No Fear Shakespeare Hamlet* 1.2.42)
thee	you (singular)	referring to a person, used as the object of the sentence "If they do see thee, they will murder thee." (*No Fear Shakespeare Romeo and Juliet* 2.2.70)
you	you (plural)	plural, used when addressing a group "Hence! Home, you idle creatures get you home!" (*No Fear Shakespeare Julius Caesar* 1.1.1)
ye	you (plural)	plural, used to address several people in high positions (formal) also used to address one or more than one person in an informal manner: "If it might please you to enforce no further / The griefs between ye, to forget them quite" (*No Fear Shakespeare Antony and Cleopatra* 2.2.107–108)
ye	the	definite article; to modify a noun in the same way *the* is used today "Ye Roman gods!" (*No Fear Shakespeare Coriolanus* 1.6.7)

Archaic Term	Modern Form	Archaic Usage Rule/Grammar
thy	your	singular—followed by a word that begins with a consonant sound

"So well thy words become thee as thy wounds[.]" (*No Fear Shakespeare Macbeth* 1.2.43) |
| **thine** | your | indicates ownership or possession; usually singular followed by a word that begins with a vowel sound

"By giving liberty unto thine eyes;" (*No Fear Shakespeare Romeo and Juliet* 1.1.217) |

Common Verbs

Archaic Term	Modern Form
'tis	it is
'twas	it was
'twere	it were
'twix	between two things; betwixt
art	are
doth	do
durst	dared
hast	have
hath	have
wilt	will

Note: Verbs ending in -est are related to the second-person pronoun *thou*.

Review the following chart. Fill in the fourth column with modern synonyms, idioms, or colloquial expressions for each archaic word or phrase provided.

Greetings, Common Words, and Expressions

Archaic Word or Phrase	Modern Form	Informal Definition	Modern Synonyms
adieu	goodbye	bye	
alack/alas	expression of sorrow often an exclamation	oh, no	
anon	in a little while, at once	in a second	
ay (aye)	yes—affirmative response	yes	
doff	to take off or remove or rid oneself of	take off	
ere	before	before	
fie	an exclamation to express disgust	Seriously?	
God ye good morrow; God ye good den (good den); God ye good e'en	good morning / good day / good evening	hello	
hie	to go quickly	hurry up	

*sparkteach

Archaic Word or Phrase	Modern Form	Informal Definition	Modern Synonyms
hither **thither**	to this place, here to that place, there	here there	
how now	How are you?	hello	
naught	nothing	all for nothing	
nay	no—negative response	No	
sirrah	used to address a servant or a person of lower stature	N/A	
whence	from where	from where	
wherefore	why	why	
withal	together	together	
yea	yes—affirmative response	yes	
yonder	in the distance	over there	

Shakespearean Stage Directions

Overview

Shakespeare often directed and acted in his plays. He wrote with an actor's sensibility and with an understanding that he would be there to guide the drama. Therefore, Shakespeare offers very little in the way of stage directions compared to modern playwrights. However, there are some consistent stage directions that Shakespeare did use, which this handout explains. Understanding these directions will help students better visualize the action of the play as they read.

Shakespearean Stage Directions

Shakespeare often directed and acted in his plays. He wrote with an actor's sensibility and with an understanding that he would be there to guide the drama. Therefore, Shakespeare offers very little in the way of stage directions compared to modern playwrights and even some of his contemporaries. In fact, Shakespeare embeds most of the characters' actions within the language of the play, leaving it up to the reader and director to decipher a character's motivation, attitude, or actions based on the inferences provided in the dialogue itself. However, there are some common stage directions Shakespeare does include that should be understood by the modern reader. The following is a list of commonly occurring stage directions in Shakespeare's plays.

Coming and Going

The most common stage directions in any play are used to indicate the coming and going of characters. Shakespeare uses simple directions to indicate such action.

Enter: indicates the entrance of a character or characters onto the stage

Exit: indicates a character exiting the stage

Exeunt: indicates the exit of multiple characters from the stage (Exeunt is Latin, the archaic third-person plural form of "exit." The term's literal translation is "they leave.")

Re-enter: indicates that a character that has recently exited the stage has returned to it

Important Moments

The entrance of an important character, such as a prince or king, and important moments like a battle are often announced with a particular flair or fanfare. The following indicators are used to highlight important characters or events.

Alarum: an archaic form of alarm used to indicate a battle is about to occur

Flourish: indicates the playing of drums and trumpets, which is used to indicate the entrance of a king

Sennet: similar to a flourish, a trumpet call signaling a group of people proceeding across the stage

Hautboys / Cornet / Trumpet: indicates that wind instruments are played to highlight or announce an important character's entrance or some other fanfare

Drum: indicates the playing of a drum

Staging

Staging, an essential element in any production, is the manner in which a play is presented on stage. Some critics believe that some of the more precise stage directions were added to Shakespeare's plays when published after his death. However, regardless of their origin, the plays offer some direction regarding movement and direction of characters or action on and around the stage. Since most of Shakespeare's plays were staged in his Globe Theatre, some of the stage directions in his plays refer specifically to the unique setup of this space.

Above / Balcony: indicates the action or direction takes place above the stage; this would indicate the use of an upper level such as one of the balconies above the stage in the Globe Theatre. The musicians would often perform from the balcony area.

Advances: the character moves forward or up to another character; sometimes indicates an aggressive action

Aside: suggests that the character speaks his or her thoughts and inner feelings directly to the audience without revealing them to the other characters on the stage; this narrative technique allows for a deeper understanding of a character's motivations and actions and is often used to create dramatic irony, revealing details to the audience that the characters on the stage are unaware of

Arras: refers to the curtain or tapestry on the stage, such as the one Polonius hides behind when he is killed by Hamlet

Below: Shakespeare's Globe Theatre was known to have a trapdoor embedded in the stage. While actors would refer to this door as "hell," stage directions refer to this area as "below." The action might also take place off the stage, where the audience traditionally stands.

Excursion: indicates a battle or fight occurring on the stage; this usually is shown by a group of people fighting across the stage or in the scene's background

Severally: the archaic equivalent of separately; indicates that actors enter from several different areas of the stage

Torches: suggests that the characters entering the stage are carrying lit torches

Within: indicates that the character speaking or being spoken to is offstage; in the context of the story, the character may be in another room or area calling to the character on the stage

More Complex Action

Shakespeare is often vague when it comes to complicated interactions. For example, in *Romeo and Juliet* the fight scenes between Tybalt and Mercutio, as well as between Romeo and Tybalt—scenes meant to convey the highest point of action in the play—are described with two simple words: "They fight."

Alternatively, Shakespeare's plays, at times, offer some rather clear direction, such as when, in *The Winter's Tale*, stage directions indicate that Antigonus "Exit[s], pursued by bear."

Basic Structural Elements

When reading Shakespeare, it is also important to understand some basic structural elements in his plays. These elements divide up the plot, pace the action, provide opportunities for settings to be changed, and make it easier for the audience to follow along.

Act: Shakespeare's plays are always divided into five acts. This structure was influenced by the Roman playwright Seneca and Aristotle's *Poetics* and forms the basic structure of Shakespeare's plays. The five-act pattern creates a basic story arc, where act one presents the exposition, act two develops the conflict, act three usually imparts the highest point of action or brings the conflict to a climactic moment, act four begins the falling action, and act five delivers the resolution.

Scene: Each act in Shakespeare's plays is divided into scenes. These divisions are often based on the place and time of the action in the scene. Most scenes will take place in one location and focus on a single set of characters.

Dramatis personae: a list of characters that appears at the beginning of the play's manuscript

Prologue: an introduction to the play recited by a single actor referred to as the chorus; the purpose of the chorus and prologue is to fill in expository, or background, information.

Epilogue: a short commentary regarding the meaning of the play spoken at the end, usually by a character reflecting on the play's events

Film Terms

Overview

Film can be an effective means of helping your students engage with literature, particularly more traditionally difficult texts, such as Shakespearean plays. Film is also an important medium for visual learners, who often appreciate seeing literature come to life on screen. This handout gives definitions for common film terms so that students can more effectively discuss the art of filmmaking and compare and contrast films with written texts to deepen their understanding and analysis of literary works.

Film Terms

Term	Definition / Explanation
background	events and images in the rear of the stage or back of the scene
blocking	figuring out or planning where actors move or stand on the stage or set

setting the camera in a particular place to capture character placement, lighting arrangement, and movement |
| **building a scene or building suspense in a scene** | using a device, such as intensifying music, to increase a scene's pace or suspense and bring it toward a climactic moment |
| **camera angle** | the point of view or perspective of the camera from which the scene is shot

Camera angles are described using the direction from which the shot is taken relative to the action, such as *low, high, neutral,* and *long shot.* Some specific shot terms include the following:

aerial shot: a shot filmed from high above using a crane, plane, or drone

boom shot: a shot taken from a high angle and sometimes involving movement of the camera

close-up shot: a shot for which the camera is zoomed in, showing the subject's head or an object at close range

dolly shot: a shot using a steadying device, such as a dolly or truck, to move the camera toward or away from the action

long shot: a shot taken from far away, designed to make a person seem small compared to the background

medium shot: a shot showing a person from the waist up

pan: to move the camera either left or right across an area

Note: *Panning* only refers to long horizontal movements in one direction.

point of view shot: a shot that shows the world through a character's perspective

tilt: the vertical version of panning—to move the camera either up or down

tracking shot: a shot following a subject while the subject is in motion

zoom: a stationary shot that zooms in or out from a subject, creating the feeling that the camera is moving |
cast	the actors and performers that appear in the film
choreographer	the person responsible for coming up with and directing organized sequences of action and movement in the film or on a stage
choreography	the directing of organized sequences of action and movement, such as fighting or dancing, in a film or on the stage

Term	Definition / Explanation
cinematography	the art of capturing images or sequences on film, specifically in reference to the use of lighting, camera angles, imagery, lenses, and blocking to artistically capture a scene
coda	a final image that functions as an epilogue for the film
composition	the organization or arrangement of shapes, lines, color, movement, and lighting the way a scene is visually constructed for effect
contrast	stark differences usually created by light and shadow
costuming / wardrobe	the costumes actors wear in a film Note: The style and period of clothing and accessories can create verisimilitude (the presence of reality in fiction) and helps to establish mood and atmosphere.
cut / editing and transitions	a sudden change in camera angle, location, scene (i.e., cutting from one scene to another) the director or film editor literally cutting film and splicing it together in certain ways to create a clear and effective action sequence Note: There are many types of cuts. The type of cut refers to the way in which the director splices scenes together. Some examples: **cross-cutting:** usually used to create action by cutting between two events in the same location. The scene's focus moves back and forth between two or more characters to build suspense. **dissolve:** when one image gradually fades out while transitioning to another **fade in / out:** the image slowly fades into the scene or fades out to, usually, a black screen **jump cut:** a quick jump between two similar but different camera angles focused on the same subject in order to give the effect of the subject or time jumping forward **montage:** a series of shots edited together to show the passage of time **wipe:** one image or scene is pushed off the side of the screen by another
director	the person who guides the action and creation of the film at all levels of production, who is responsible for telling the story, and who is credited for the film as an author would be credited for writing a book There are often many directors on a film set who specialize in certain areas of production, such as the director of photography, the music director, etc.
editing	the post-filming process of arranging, cutting, and structuring the film to create a complete and cohesive story
fade	when an image or music fades in or out of a scene, or when a scene fades from darkness to light or sound to silence
filter	device used to change the lighting in a film to create a specific effect or atmosphere
focus	the sharpness or distortion of an image created by the manipulation of a camera lens

*sparkteach 47

Term	Definition / Explanation
foreground	where a scene's main action occurs
fourth wall	a term that refers to the audience Note: The term is often used when characters "break" the fourth wall and talk directly to the audience.
frame	what is captured by the camera in a single image
genre	the style or type of film, based on thematic or plot elements Some genre examples are musicals, westerns, horror, romantic comedy, and action adventure.
juxtaposition	the positioning of two images, characters, objects, or scenes together for the purpose of comparison Juxtaposition establishes stark contrast or relationships between two characters or scenes.
lighting	the manipulation of light and darkness used by the cinematographer to create mood and atmosphere Some specific types of lighting include the following: *backlighting*: the subject is lit from behind, creating a shadow or silhouette for the camera *fill light*: a light is placed to the side of an actor or scene in order to eliminate shadows in the background of the scene *key light*: the central or main lighting for a scene *mood lighting*: lighting used to create a particular mood or atmosphere; usually involves colored lights and shadows
location	the place where the scene is filmed
makeup	the use of cosmetics, costuming, masks, and other elements to enhance or distort human features Makeup artists are responsible for everything from simple beauty makeup to the design and development of creatures and monsters.
mise en scène	backdrop, sets, props, actors, and lighting This French term literally translates to "placing on stage."
motif	a recurring image or idea in a film
props	an object used in a scene (shortened from "theatrical property")
scene	many shots taken in a single location that focus on a single action
script	the text containing the dialogue and story for the film
set	the stage or stages in which the actions for the film are recorded

Term	Definition / Explanation
soundtrack	the music written for or played during various film sequences Music enhances mood and atmosphere.
special effects	illusions and visual tricks used to create impossible images, objects, or events Note: Most special effects today are created by CGI (computer generated images), but there are still many mechanical and nondigital optical illusions used to create special effects.
tone	the way a film "feels" or how a film is supposed to make the audience feel Tone is set through the mood and atmosphere of the film. The tone of a film can be humorous, serious, shocking, satiric, sad, etc.

*sparkteach

Metaphor and Simile

Overview

Metaphor and simile are two of the most commonly taught, studied, and tested literary devices. Understanding these prolific devices will enable students to more fully understand and appreciate great works of literature. Students will use this worksheet to learn about metaphors and similes and the distinctions between them. They will then dissect examples of each from notable works of literature.

RL.9-10.4 Determine the meaning of words and phrases as they are used in the text, including figurative and connotative meanings; analyze the cumulative impact of specific word choices on meaning and tone (e.g., how the language evokes a sense of time and place; how it sets a formal or informal tone).

Metaphor and Simile

Abstractions by definition are difficult to understand. Since the purpose of literature in all of its forms is, ultimately, to convey some abstract concept about the human condition in a meaningful manner, writers often employ literary and poetic devices that make the abstract qualities of life's experiences concrete and relatable to a reader. Abstract concepts like *love*, *jealousy*, *fear*, and *hate* have many complex and nuanced characteristics. In order to clearly convey these concepts, writers often rely on comparisons in the form of figurative language. Two of the most commonly used forms of figurative language are metaphor and simile.

1. Understand the terms.

    A metaphor is a direct comparison of two unlike things. A metaphor is presented through words or phrases that are not literally true.

    A simile functions the same way as a metaphor, but the comparison is made through the use of words such as *like*, *as*, *than*, and *so*.

2. Practice making abstract connections: Choose an abstract idea from the following list and create similes by relating the idea to something concrete, yet seemingly unrelated to the abstraction. Then explain why the two elements are similar.

Abstractions: *love, hate, jealousy, anger, fear, excitement, hardship, peace, family, prejudice*
Use the following template to develop the simile:

(**Abstract idea**) is like (**concrete element**) because (**explanation**).

For example: **Love** is like **a bacon cheeseburger** because **it is fulfilling and delicious but can sometimes lead to unforeseen problems.**

_____ is like _____ because _____ .

_____ is like _____ because _____ .

_____ is like _____ because _____ .

_____ is like _____ because _____ .

*spark teach   51

3. Explain the comparison created by the following metaphors and similes. First, explain the abstract idea and the concrete element it is being compared to. Then explain the concept conveyed by the comparison.

What happens **to a dream deferred**?

Does it dry up

Like **a raisin in the sun**?

(from "Harlem" by Langston Hughes)

Abstract Idea	Concrete Element	Relationship: (abstract idea) **is like** (concrete element) **because . . .**
a dream deferred	a raisin in the sun	A dream deferred is like a raisin in the sun because

All the **world's a stage**, And all the **men and women** merely **players**[.]

(from *As You Like It* by William Shakespeare)

Abstract Idea	Concrete Element	Relationship: (abstract idea) **is like** (concrete element) **because . . .**
world	stage	A world is like a stage because
men and women	players	

*sparkteach

The **bank**—the **monster** has to have profits all the time. It can't wait. It'll die.

(from *The Grapes of Wrath* by John Steinbeck)

Abstract Idea	Concrete Element	Relationship: (abstract idea) **is like** (concrete element) **because . . .**
bank	monster	

4. Now it's your turn! Identify the abstract and concrete comparable elements in the examples, and then explain how the abstract idea and concrete element are alike.

I wandered lonely as a cloud

That floats on high o'er vales and hills[.]

(from "I Wandered Lonely as a Cloud" by William Wordsworth)

Abstract Idea	Concrete Element	Relationship: (abstract idea) is like (concrete element) because . . .

Let us go then, you and I,

When the evening is spread out against the sky

Like a patient etherized upon a table[.]

(from "The Love Song of J. Alfred Prufrock" by T.S. Eliot)

Abstract Idea	Concrete Element	Relationship: (abstract idea) is like (concrete element) because . . .

5. For one final challenge, try to identify the abstract and concrete ideas in this extended passage and explain the relationships created through the metaphoric comparison.

> And that night there came on a terrific storm, with driving rain, awful claps of thunder and blinding sheets of lightning. He covered his head with the bed-clothes and waited in a horror of suspense for his doom; for he had not the shadow of a doubt that all this hubbub was about him. He believed he had taxed the forbearance of the powers above to the extremity of endurance and that this was the result. It might have seemed to him a waste of pomp and ammunition to kill a bug with a battery of artillery, but there seemed nothing incongruous about the getting up such an expensive thunderstorm as this to knock the turf from under an insect like himself.

(from *The Adventures of Tom Sawyer* by Mark Twain)

Abstract Idea	Concrete Element	Relationship: (abstract idea) is like (concrete element) because . . .

Abstract Idea	Concrete Element	Relationship: (abstract idea) is like (concrete element) because . . .

Dreams and Dreaming: The Search for Understanding

Overview

Dreams play a major role in *A Midsummer Night's Dream*—both as a theme and as a literary device Shakespeare uses to explore the nature of reality. The subject of dreams was no less captivating and mysterious in Shakespeare's time than it is today. This handout gives students important background information on dreams and dreaming in the sixteenth century, beginning with a brief overview of the history of the art of dream interpretation in human culture; evidence of how this art was alive and well in Shakespeare's time; and how the topic continues to be explored today with Sigmund Freud's *The Interpretation of Dreams*. Students are also given a brief overview of recent scientific theories about how and why we dream. Use this handout to spark discussion and debate in your classroom and allow students to express their own personal experiences and theories related to dreams and dreaming.

RL.9-10.1 Cite strong and thorough textual evidence to support analysis of what the text says explicitly as well as inferences drawn from the text.

RL.9-10.2 Determine a theme or central idea of a text and analyze in detail its development over the course of the text, including how it emerges and is shaped and refined by specific details; provide an objective summary of the text.

Dreams and Dreaming: The Search for Understanding

What Are Dreams?

In Renaissance England, people were as captivated by the mysterious nature of dreams and the act of dreaming as they are today. They asked the same questions as we do now: *Where do dreams come from? What do dreams mean? How should dreams be interpreted, if at all?* Even as today's science and technology promises to "unlock the code" of dreaming by understanding the biological and psychological processes behind dreaming, definitive answers to these questions still remain (tantalizingly) out of reach.

Early Dream Interpretation

As far back as the third millennium BCE, Mesopotamian kings were known to record their dreams on clay tablets, suggesting that even then people were aware that dreams held at least some importance and relevance to daily life. Ancient Egyptians were one of the first cultures to attempt to systematize the interpretation of dreams by creating a "dream book" that listed over one hundred common dreams and their meanings. According to this ancient culture, the gods spoke to humans through dreams, and interpreting dreams was a divine practice reserved for those with special training.

Classical and Medieval Dream Interpretation

The art of "divining" the true meaning of dreams continued through the medieval and classical eras. Within this religious context, the art of discerning and interpreting dreams became a matter of separating the authentic from the bogus. After all, if God really did communicate through dreams, then it was of the utmost importance to be able to tell which dreams truly were divine and who were the people worthy and virtuous enough to receive them. Furthermore, whoever had the power to unlock a dream's meaning was of special interest to political and military leaders looking for solutions to complicated problems and special advantages in war. For many, dreams were thought to be the same as prophecies.

Dreams in Elizabethan England

In Shakespeare's time, Thomas Hill's *The Most Pleasant Art of the Interpretation of Dreams* (1576) was the most comprehensive text on dream theory and interpretation. Hill's text laid out the history of dreams and dream interpretation through the ages and reflected the general anxieties Elizabethans had over dreams at the time. Hill acknowledged that the art of dream interpretation was indeed complicated and approached the subject with a fair degree of skepticism and balance. Elizabethans were especially concerned with sleep dynamics both physical and psychological. They pondered questions like, *How vulnerable was one to supernatural forces while asleep? Is it possible to control dreams so that one is visited only by angels, and not demons? Could one's bad character be "exposed" through dreams*? Shakespeare plays on these ideas in his works, as he has characters experience prophetic dreams, have their guilt exposed, and manipulate others through dreaming and the dream state.

Are Dreams Just . . . Dreams?

Even as these loftier ideas were discussed, more mundane theories about dreams persisted. Some of these ideas extended as far back as to Aristotle, who suggested that dreams were the result of simple biological functions. Some Elizabethans considered dreams a simple yet stranger "retelling" of the day's events. Still others reserved judgment and sought to control their dreams through healthy diet and prayer and used such strategies as wearing gemstones or drinking special potions before bed to stay on the safe side and avoid nightmares.

Freud's The Interpretation of Dreams

Today, Sigmund Freud's *The Interpretation of Dreams* (1899) has replaced Hill's text to become the most recent comprehensive exploration of dreaming and dream interpretation. Freud's provocative proposal suggests that we dream to achieve a level of "wish fulfillment," meaning that our dreams represent desires we have not yet achieved in "real life," so we manifest or obtain these goals in the dream state. Dreams then, Freud argues, become a larger picture of our unmet and/or repressed desires. Freud also suggests dreams are a collection of images from our daily conscious mind that have symbolic meanings that correspond to our subconscious, primitive mind. He argues that if we can decode the symbolic meaning of these images, we can unlock our repressed desires, and therefore make the subconscious known, leading us toward psychological unification and healing.

The Science of Dreaming

Psychological studies since Freud offer even more explanations for why we dream and what dreams mean. Some theories propose that certain memory processes can happen only while we are asleep and that dreams are a simple biological by-product of the storing and consolidation of memories. Other theories propose that dreams act like a "sieve" for the plethora of neural connections we make during the day that we no longer need and which could clog up our brains. Some other theories acknowledge that these biological-based explanations are not sufficient. These theories suggest that much remains ambiguous about dreams, even as they point to the possible emotional and potentially healing value of dreams. Thus, despite our long search for answers about dreaming, it remains a mysteriously elusive part of the human experience

Poetic Wordplay

Overview

Shakespeare is considered by many literary scholars to be the master at manipulating language. Even centuries after his death, he sets a standard for rich writing that few, if any, can match. Shakespeare uses a number of literary techniques to create complex language that engages readers and layers meaning. Students will use this worksheet to explore how Shakespeare uses wordplay, particularly puns, to add meaning and humor to *A Midsummer Night's Dream*. They may work independently, in pairs, or as a class to complete this worksheet.

RL.11-12.4 Determine the meaning of words and phrases as they are used in the text, including figurative and connotative meanings; analyze the impact of specific word choices on meaning and tone, including words with multiple meanings or language that is particularly fresh, engaging, or beautiful. (Include Shakespeare as well as other authors.)

L.11-12.4 Determine or clarify the meaning of unknown and multiple-meaning words and phrases based on grades 11–12 reading and content, choosing flexibly from a range of strategies.

L.11-12.5 Demonstrate understanding of figurative language, word relationships, and nuances in word meanings.

Poetic Wordplay

Any good writer will create rich, complex language that engages readers and layers meaning. Shakespeare is considered by many literary scholars to be the master at manipulating language. Even centuries after his death, he sets a standard for rich writing that few, if any, can match. Shakespeare used an arsenal of literary devices to craft the language in his plays, and puns are one of the most frequently found elements in his writing.

> **A pun is a form of wordplay in which a writer "plays" with the multiple meanings of a single word or uses two similar-sounding words with different meanings to create an effect (usually humor).**

In *A Midsummer Night's Dream*, Shakespeare relies heavily on puns to amuse readers and underscore some of the play's major themes.

In rows 1 and 2: Read the term and a pun that uses the term from *A Midsummer Night's Dream*. Review the connotative and denotative meanings of the term, the effect the pun creates, and the relationship between the pun and the play's themes.

In rows 3 and 4: Record two additional examples of puns from the play. Be sure to fill in all of the columns for each of your examples.

Term	Pun	Connotative Meaning(s)
lie	Hermia: Lie further off yet, do not lie so near. Lysander: Then by your side no bed room me deny, For lying so, Hermia, I do not lie. (*No Fear*: 2.2.33–41)	to recline; to say something false
ass	Bottom: What do you see? You see an ass head of your own, do you? . . . I see their knavery: this is to make an ass of me, to fright me if they could. (*No Fear*: 3.1.56–58)	a foolish person; a donkey

Denotative Meaning(s)	Effect	Relationship to Play's Themes
Hermia asks Lysander to not lie so close to her but is also saying don't tell her lies while lying so close to her. Lysander insists he wasn't implying he wanted to sleep with her.	humor, playfulness	highlights the themes of nonsense and playfulness
Bottom's head has been changed into the head of a donkey by Puck, causing the others to run away scared. Bottom says they must be seeing their own ass-headedness in themselves, or they are trying to make an ass of him by scaring him.	humor, mischief	highlights the theme of human folly but also the wisdom of fools since Bottom's statement is wise

*sparkteach

Order and Chaos

Overview

Understanding major themes and identifying how they are reflected in character and plot is an essential skill for literary analysis. The states of order and chaos play important roles throughout Shakespeare's *A Midsummer Night's Dream*. Students will use this worksheet to examine the text in terms of order and chaos, summarize how the plot's key action roughly falls into these two major categories, and ultimately determine who or what is the cause of the order and chaos in the play. Pass out this worksheet before students begin reading the play and have them return to it after they read each act.

RL.11-12.2 Determine two or more themes or central ideas of a text and analyze their development over the course of the text, including how they interact and build on one another to produce a complex account; provide an objective summary of the text.

Order and Chaos

Much of the action in *A Midsummer Night's Dream* falls into the category of either order or chaos. Shakespeare uses characters, setting, plot, and other devices to create these two opposing forces in the play. Fill out the graphic organizer to summarize each of the play's five acts in terms of order and chaos. Think about who or what is responsible for order and chaos in the play. After you've completed the graphic organizer, answer the questions that follow.

Act 1: Order

The play opens in Athens. Theseus is happily planning his wedding to Hippolyta. Hermia and Lysander are in love.

↓

Act 1: Chaos

Act 2: Order

↓

Act 2: Chaos

↓

Act 3: Order

↓

Act 3: Chaos

Act 4: Order

Act 4: Chaos

Act 5: Order

Act 5: Chaos

1. Who or what causes order in the play? How?

2. Who or what causes chaos in the play? How?

3. Who or what causes both order and chaos in the play? How?

Exploring Theme: Dreams

Overview

Identifying themes and their relationships to one another form a foundation for understanding a work of literature. Shakespeare weaves the theme of dreams and dreaming throughout *A Midsummer Night's Dream*. Students will use this worksheet to analyze how this theme relates to other major themes in the play, including love, marriage, gender, and friendship. Students will detail how Shakespeare uses character, setting, and plot to develop each of these themes and how he builds upon each one to create a larger message about the nature of dreams. Students will then summarize their findings in a paragraph (or longer) written response.

RL.11-12.1 Cite strong and thorough textual evidence to support analysis of what the text says explicitly as well as inferences drawn from the text, including determining where the text leaves matters uncertain.

RL.11-12.2 Determine two or more themes or central ideas of a text and analyze their development over the course of the text, including how they interact and build on one another to produce a complex account; provide an objective summary of the text.

Exploring Theme: Dreams

Dreams comprise a major theme in Shakespeare's *A Midsummer Night's Dream*. The act of dreaming, nightmares, dreams representing wishes and desires, dreams blurring one's understanding of reality—these are just some of the dream-related concepts Shakespeare explores in the play.

Use the graphic organizer to map how the theme of dreams relates to four additional themes in the play—love, marriage, gender, and friendship. Use the boxes to break down how Shakespeare builds these themes through three major literary elements: character, setting, and plot. Then, write a response to the prompt below:

How does the theme of dreams relate to the play's other themes of love, marriage, gender, and friendship? What statement is Shakespeare making about the nature of dreams through these themes?

Love

Characters:
Demetrius's love for Helena seems to awaken in a dream or spell.

Setting:
The forest becomes a dream-like atmosphere where the characters explore their love.

Plot:
Dreams cause the characters to view their love irrationally and act in a bizarre way.

Marriage

Characters:

Setting:

Plot:

DREAMS

Gender

Characters:

Setting:

Plot:

Friendship

Characters:

Setting:

Plot:

*spark teach

Dreamer or Realist?

Overview

Much of what an author has to say about a particular theme is revealed through the thoughts and words of major characters. In *A Midsummer Night's Dream*, each character has something to say on the topic of dreams and reality that reflects his or her perspectives, beliefs, and worldviews. Students will use this worksheet to locate and examine important quotes from the play in which characters discuss dreams and analyze what larger message about dreams and reality Shakespeare sends through the mouths of his characters.

RL.11-12.1 Cite strong and thorough textual evidence to support analysis of what the text says explicitly as well as inferences drawn from the text, including determining where the text leaves matters uncertain.

RL.11-12.3 Analyze the impact of the author's choices regarding how to develop and relate elements of a story or drama (e.g., where a story is set, how the action is ordered, how the characters are introduced and developed).

Dreamer or Realist?

1. Every character in *A Midsummer Night's Dream* has something to say about dreams, imagination, and the nature of reality. Through these characters, Shakespeare creates an array of opinions to develop and explore these themes. Some characters are open to the idea that reality might not be what it seems, whereas others are not.

2. **In column 2**: Record a quote spoken by the character from column 1 in which he or she discusses or muses on dreams and dreaming. Remember to cite the quote's location in the text. Beneath each quote, write one or two sentences explaining the quote's meaning.

3. **In column 3**: Explain whether this character is a dreamer, a realist, or both.

4. After you've completed the chart, respond to the prompt below.

Character	Quote	Dreamer or Realist?
Theseus	"More strange than true. I never may believe These antique fables nor these fairy toys." (*No Fear*: 5.1.2–3) Theseus is saying that he doesn't believe the strange tales that Hermia and the others are telling about their night in the forest. He doesn't believe in stories and "fairy toys."	Theseus seems like a realist. He doesn't entertain the idea that fairies might exist.
Hippolyta	"But all the story of the night told over, And all their minds transfigured so together, More witnesseth than fancy's images And grows to something of great constancy, But, howsoever, strange and admirable." (*No Fear*: 5.1.23–27) Hippolyta notices that the tales Hermia and the others are telling are strange, but they all seem to line up.	Hippolyta seems like a mix between a dreamer and a realist. She's not willing to dismiss the stories as made up, but she also won't say that fairies don't exist.

*sparkteach   **75**

Character	Quote	Dreamer or Realist?
Oberon		
Titania		
Puck		
Lysander		

Character	Quote	Dreamer or Realist?
Hermia		
Demetrius		
Helena		
Bottom		

Choose one character from the chart. Analyze how this character's actions and opinions help advance the theme of dreams and reality in the play.

Comedy or Tragedy?

Overview

The key elements of comedy and tragedy as described in Aristotle's *Poetics* were mainly followed by Shakespeare in his plays and are, in fact, still in use in most works of literature today. Students will use this worksheet to briefly review the dramatic conventions of comedy and tragedy as outlined in *Poetics* and to examine *A Midsummer Night's Dream* for examples of each convention. Students will then make their own assessment as to whether *A Midsummer Night's Dream* is a comedy or a tragedy. Pass out this worksheet after they finish reading the text.

RL.11-12.5 Analyze how an author's choices concerning how to structure specific parts of a text (e.g., the choice of where to begin or end a story, the choice to provide a comedic or tragic resolution) contribute to its overall structure and meaning as well as its aesthetic impact.

Comedy or Tragedy?

According to Aristotle, comedy and tragedy each follow a set of particular dramatic conventions. For the most part, Shakespeare's plays follow these conventions, though he sometimes mixes elements of each type in one play.

Review the chart that lists common elements found in comedies and tragedies. Next, in the blank charts, record the elements of comedy and the elements of tragedy in Shakespeare's *A Midsummer Night's Dream*. Then, write a paragraph assessing whether the play is a comedy or tragedy.

Elements of Comedy	Elements of Tragedy
Usually has a happy ending	Ending is usually tragic
Audience knows the conflict will resolve in a happy ending beforehand	Audience is kept in suspense; doesn't know ending beforehand
Characters have exaggerated flaws that make them seem buffoonish	Characters are usually "more admirable" than the average audience member
Characters' misfortunes and dilemmas aren't taken as seriously since audience already knows ending will be happy	Main character will have a "tragic flaw" (usually involves hubris) that inspires pity or fear in the audience
Has a lighthearted, humorous tone	Characters' suffering can seem fated or ultimately insurmountable
Satirizing, or "making low" of high-minded concepts and themes	Deals with serious themes

What elements of comedy are found in *A Midsummer Night's Dream*?

Element	Explanation
Puck turns Bottom's head into that of an ass.	This is a comedic element because it emphasizes what a buffoon Bottom is.

What elements of tragedy are found in *A Midsummer Night's Dream*?

Element	Explanation
Hermia's father is okay with her dying if she doesn't agree to marry Demetrius.	This is tragic because it is a situation that Hermia can't escape; she has no choice but to die or submit to her father's will.

Your final assessment: Is *A Midsummer Night's Dream* a comedy or tragedy?

Doubling

Overview

Doubling is a literary device an author might use to explore the dual characteristics (often contrary) of a character, place, idea, or other aspect of life. Shakespeare uses this device frequently, so it is essential for students to be able to identify it in his work and recognize how and why he uses it. Students will use this worksheet to analyze doubling in *A Midsummer Night's Dream* by comparing and contrasting humans and fairies and Athens and the fairy world.

RL.11-12.1 Cite strong and thorough textual evidence to support analysis of what the text says explicitly as well as inferences drawn from the text, including determining where the text leaves matters uncertain.

RL.11-12.2 Determine two or more themes or central ideas of a text and analyze their development over the course of the text, including how they interact and build on one another to produce a complex account; provide an objective summary of the text.

Doubling

HERMIA

When everything seems double. Methinks I see these things with parted eye.

(*No Fear*: 4.1.176)

In literature, doubling happens when two characters, places, or ideas are used to parallel one another. Doubling encourages the reader to think about the relationships between these elements, how they are interconnected, and how they represent dualities, such as good and evil, familiar and strange, or real and unreal.

Use the chart to explore the ways Shakespeare uses doubling in *A Midsummer Night's Dream*. Compare and contrast the elements connected by arrows—humans and fairies and Athens and the fairy world. Then respond to the questions below.

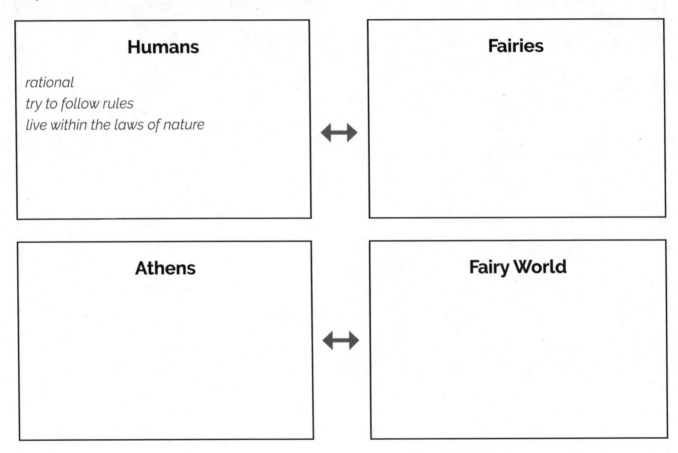

Humans

rational
try to follow rules
live within the laws of nature

Fairies

Athens

Fairy World

1. What do the fairies reflect about the humans? What do the humans reflect about the fairies?

2. What does Athens reflect about the fairy world? What does the fairy world reflect about Athens?

Driving Questions	Initial Answer	Final Answer
What happens to the characters' perceptions of reality while they are in the forest?	Text evidence:	Text evidence:
Who is under the spell of the love potion? Who isn't? Why might this be significant?	Text evidence:	Text evidence:
What does the love potion symbolize? How does it link dreams and reality?	Text evidence:	Text evidence:
What "truths" are revealed about the characters while in the forest?	Text evidence:	Text evidence:

Driving Questions	Initial Answer	Final Answer
How does Shakespeare set up an opposition between the city and the forest, and how does this relate to the theme of reality and illusion in the play?	Text evidence:	Text evidence:
How does dreaming function as both a disruptive and unifying force in the play?	Text evidence:	Text evidence:
What are Theseus's views on love and rationality, and how are they similar to or different from Hermia's?	Text evidence:	Text evidence:
How do Theseus's and Hermia's views together form a "complete" commentary on reality in the play?	Text evidence:	Text evidence:
Why do you think Shakespeare chooses dreams as a literary device?	Text evidence:	Text evidence:

The Dream in the Forest

Character	Before the Forest	In the Forest	Out of the Forest
Hermia			
Lysander			
Demetrius			
Helena			
Bottom			

Poetic Meter and Social Class

Complete the chart below with one example of verse and one of prose from the play.

In column 1: Record the character's name.

In column 2: Record the social class of the character.

In column 3: Record a quote from the text spoken by the character. Cite the location in the text.

In column 4: State if the character speaks in verse or prose. If verse, try to identify the meter.

In column 5: Briefly explain what effect is created by the kind of language spoken by the character.

Character	Social Class	Passage from Text	Type of Language	Effect
Hermia	nobility	"So will I grow, so live, so die, my lord, Ere I will yield my virgin patent up[.]" (*No Fear*: 1.1.79–80)	verse – iambic pentameter	formal; expresses the seriousness of Hermia's refusal to marry against her will
Bottom	commoner	"First, good Peter Quince, say what the play treats on, then read the names of the actors, and so grow to a point." (*No Fear*: 1.2.3–4)	prose	informal/natural; casual conversation about the actors

Consider these two similar passages, and then answer the questions.

Quince:	Robin/Puck:
"If we offend, it is with our good will. That you should think we come not to offend, But with good will. To show our simple skill, That is the true beginning of our end." (*No Fear*: 5.1.103–106)	"If we shadows have offended, Think but this, and all is mended— That you have but slumbered here While these visions did appear. And this weak and idle theme, No more yielding but a dream[.]" (*No Fear*: 5.1.406–411)

1. What meter is Quince speaking in?

2. What meter is Puck speaking in?

3. How is the content of both passages similar? How is it different?

4. What effect does Shakespeare create paralleling these two passages?

Themes in Hoffman's Film

Theme	Scene in the Text	Scene in the Film	Overall Effect
Dreams	Scene: Act 1, scene 2 There is no mention of Bottom's wife and there are no kids who throw things at Bottom. The reason the performers go to practice in the forest is so that no one will know they are intending to perform a play for the Duke.	Scene: Men are practicing in the town center for the play. Bottom's wife runs into a crowd looking for him, shouting he is a "useless dreamer." Also, Bottom is humiliated by a group of children, so he and the other performers all decide to practice in the forest so they won't be bothered or seen.	The different treatment in the film causes the audience to feel compassion for Bottom. We see that Bottom is more than a foolish guy. He has dreams, and we feel bad when he is humiliated. Bottom's wife wants him to be more stable, but Bottom can't help who he is.
Love/Desire			

Theme	Scene in the Text	Scene in the Film	Overall Effect
Jealousy			
Friendship			
Social Class			

PART 4
Postmortem

After the unit, use the following Rubric for Student Assessment to assess your students' learning and the Student and Teacher Reflection worksheets to capture your experience with the Lesson Plans.

Rubric for Student Assessment

Overview

Using a rubric can help you assess students' learning more accurately and more consistently. Giving the rubric to your students before they begin a task that will be assessed also makes your expectations clear and encourages students to take responsibility for their own learning and success on an assignment. This rubric can be used across multiple midpoint activities and final projects to assess students' learning and understanding. You can also edit a version of the rubric to tailor it to specific learning goals you have for your classes.

Rubric for Student Assessment

Area of Performance	4	3	2	1
Content development	Work clearly and thoroughly addresses the prompt. All details/ideas support the main topic. Ideas are original, creative, and supported by numerous concrete details from the text.	Work mostly addresses the prompt. Most details/ideas support the main topic. A few concrete details from the text are provided.	Work doesn't stay on target and/or doesn't follow the prompt. Only a few supporting details are provided.	Work doesn't stay on target or follow the prompt. Ideas are confusing. Details are irrelevant or missing.
Organization	Details are presented in a logical and meaningful order. Essays or presentations include a clear introduction, body, and conclusion. Statements reflect critical thinking skills. Appropriate transitions are used to connect ideas.	Most details are presented in a logical order and are related to the main topic. The writing is clear, but the introduction, body, or conclusion needs strengthening.	Many details are presented in an illogical order or are unrelated to the main topic. The writing lacks a clear introduction, well-organized body, or a strong conclusion.	Details and ideas are poorly organized and unrelated to main topic.
Language and style	Writing or spoken language is smooth, coherent, and stays on topic. Sentence structure varies. Strong verbs and descriptive details and language clarify and strengthen ideas.	Writing or spoken language stays on topic but sentence structure doesn't vary. Some descriptive details are used to clarify ideas.	Some writing or spoken language doesn't flow and/or lacks creativity. Some language unrelated to or inappropriate for the main topic is used.	Writing or spoken language is confusing. Incomplete or run-on sentences are used. Many terms used are unrelated to or inappropriate for the main topic.

Area of Performance	4	3	2	1
Mechanics (when applicable)	All grammar and punctuation is correct. The writing is free of spelling errors.	The writing is mostly free of grammatical, mechanical, and spelling errors.	Writing contains several grammatical, punctuation, and spelling errors.	The writing contains numerous errors that make it difficult to understand.
Collaboration (when applicable)	Student played a valuable role in group work. Student worked well with others, listened respectfully to others' ideas, and resolved any challenges in an appropriate manner.	Student played an important role in group work but could have been more open to others' ideas and/or could have resolved challenges in a more constructive manner.	Student did minimal work in his/her group. Student ignored group challenges or left challenges unresolved.	Student didn't do her/his fair share of work. Student did not engage in the group task.
Research (when applicable)	Multiple, reliable sources were used to gather information. All sources are properly cited or credited.	Some research was done to complete the task. Not all sources are cited or some citations are incomplete.	Little or no research was done to gather necessary information. No sources are cited.	No research was done.

Student and Teacher Reflection Worksheets

Overview

A reflective practice helps you continue to develop new and engaging teaching strategies that meet the needs of all students in your class. Tracking successes as well as challenges throughout a unit of study also decreases planning time for future classes and helps you tailor your lessons to improve each time you teach them. Use this worksheet to reflect on a Real-Life Lens Lesson you have taught and record what was successful and what you would change when you teach the material again. Make notes on interesting ideas you added to the Lens Lesson or thoughts your students had that inspired you along the way.

Student Reflection Worksheet

1. How did reading the text through the lens of dreams and reality affect your engagement with and understanding of this text?

   _____

   _____

   _____

2. What difficulties did you encounter with this text, and how did you address them?

   _____

   _____

   _____

3. Consider the Real-Life Links you encountered at the beginning of the lesson. Which resources did you find the most interesting? Why?

   _____

   _____

4. How effective were the Driving Questions in guiding you to a deeper understanding of the text?

   _____

   _____

   _____

5. Describe one challenge you faced while working on an activity or project and how you overcame it.

   _____

   _____

   _____

6. What new insight or skill did you take away from this lesson?

   _____

   _____

   _____